PICTURES · FROM · THE · PAST

The Seaside

PICTURES · FROM · THE · PAST

The Seaside

Gavin Weightman

First published in Great Britain in 1991
by Collins & Brown Limited

Text Copyright © Gavin Weightman 1991

A CIP catalogue record for this book
is available from the British Library

ISBN 1 85585 082 6

The pictures in this book are archive photographs and, to preserve the character and
quality of the original, have not been re-touched in any way.

Acknowledgements
The author and publishers are grateful to Southend-on-Sea Museums Service for
permission to reproduce the following copyright photographs on pages 80 (top left) and
85 (top right).

All other photographs were supplied by the Hulton Picture Company and are available as
framed prints. For more information and to place your orders contact:

Framed Prints
Hulton Picture Company
Unique House
21–31 Woodfield Road
London W9 2BA

Tel: 071 266 2660
Fax: 071 266 2414

Conceived, edited and designed by Collins & Brown Limited,
Mercury House, 195 Knightsbridge, London SW7 1RE

Editor: Sarah Hoggett
Picture Research: Philippa Lewis
Art Director: Roger Bristow
Designed by: Gail Jones and Sally Smallwood

Filmset by Tradespools Ltd, Frome
Reproduction by Scantrans, Singapore
Printed and bound in Great Britain by Butler & Tanner Ltd, Frome

CONTENTS

INTRODUCTION

The rise and decline of the seaside holiday is one of the most amusing sagas in British social history. The very names of resorts – Bournemouth, Blackpool, Bognor Regis, Skegness, or Scarborough – have a mildly comical air today, redolent of a now outmoded way of having fun which was once shockingly new. Three million people still go to Blackpool and more than a million visit Bournemouth each year; and the bucket-and-spade holiday, spent behind a windbreak on a dank beach, is far from dead. But the golden age of the English seaside is well and truly over. Rusting piers and crumbling promenades are testimony to that. The rise in sun-bathing and package holidays abroad undermined the prosperity of the chillier British coast, while the motor car and television have taken away much of the flavour of seaside entertainment.

BELOW: *The Edwardian seafront at Scarborough, one of the oldest resorts, which had also been an eighteenth-century spa. People once* drank *the sea water here as a cure for glandular troubles.*

Happily, however, the long-established enthusiasm for holiday photographs has preserved a good deal of the flavour of the seaside in its heyday. They capture the British, in different eras, behaving, in a sense, out of character, for it was always remarked that there was something about being by the seaside that was liberating to the spirit. It was where people might – horror of horrors – take their clothes off in public, drink too much and play the fool. Despite the impression given by some of the earlier photographs of ridiculously over-dressed and drab-looking people on the beach, the seaside was considered to be a serious threat by Victorian moralists.

The fashion for sea-bathing began in the eighteenth century, when it was regarded more as a form of therapy than enjoyment. The seaside resort was a successor to the inland spas – such as Bath or Wells – which evolved from earlier religious pilgrimages to sources of holy water. Early on, in the late sixteenth and early seventeenth centuries, doctors recommended

the drinking of sea water. Remarkably, that is what the well-to-do health enthusiast did. Bathing became popular in the 1720s and the first bathing machines were trundled into the sea at Scarborough, which was also a fresh water spa, in 1735.

Bathing in the nude was common then, and was still frequently remarked upon in the 1860s. A bathing machine, if you could afford one, provided a degree of privacy when swimming costumes were cumbersome. In many places, men and women had separate bathing areas on the beach, but a great deal of amusement could be had from the seafront with a pair of opera glasses. Mixed bathing and more convenient costumes arrived in the later nineteenth century, but even then a great many people who could not afford them simply took off their shoes and paddled. The British holidaymaker standing in the sea with trousers rolled up or skirt raised is an abiding image.

Until the railways were built from the 1830s onwards only the well-to-do had the time and money to travel far to resorts. But from the Lancashire towns cotton workers would walk to Blackpool which was becoming a popular resort in the early 1800s. During the Victorian period, the railways and steamers with cheap excursion fares made many resorts accessible to large numbers of working people, and a kind of snobbish league table of resorts arose. The flight of the genteel classes to the more distant and quiet resorts began.

Some seaside amusements – notably the bucket and spade, donkey rides and the building of sandcastles – have endured. But the late Victorian and Edwardian atmosphere in resorts was very different from anything found today. Fine weather was naturally pleasing, but nobody went for the sun; the chief health attraction was the bracing air. The medical profession, whose powers of invention were always inversely proportional to their understanding of illness, claimed to be able to detect special medicinal properties in the air of different resorts.

LEFT: *Bathing machines at Bexhill-on-Sea around 1900. Mixed bathing was introduced here in 1902. Within a few years, swimmers changed in tents on the beach.*

BELOW: *Paddling at Clacton in 1922. A great many holidaymakers got no further into the sea than this.*

But the real cure of the seaside was enjoyment, and the entertainment industry followed the crowds to the coast. A great deal of fun was to be had on the beach with Punch and Judy shows, 'nigger minstrels', clowns or pierrots and a variety of bands. The larger and more down-market resorts like Blackpool, with the aid of electricity, established funfairs and the famous illuminations in the 1880s. Rhyl in North Wales, popular with people from the Potteries, opened its Winter Gardens in the 1870s, with a skating rink, theatre and zoo; and in 1902 it constructed an artificial subterranean Venice with gondolas.

In the nineteenth century a great many visitors to the seaside were day-trippers. Only small sections of the working class had holidays as such, and fewer had paid holidays. The creation of Bank Holidays in 1871 produced a startling outpouring of people to the coast in August. Bit by bit, more and more people could take a week off in the year, but it was not until 1938 that the right to a paid holiday became established in law, and this could not be enjoyed by most people until after the war. The seaside thus had its most buoyant time in the late 1940s and early 1950s.

While railways provided the chief means of getting to the coast, the social segregation between the tiddly-om-pom-pom of the Blackpools and the sedate breezy promenades of the Bournemouths could be sustained. But first the charabanc and then, after the 1950s, the motor car made the more isolated places accessible. To the horror of those who had maintained the quiet, studious and therapeutic view of the seaside, the caravan began to appear in select little coves. The smallest fishing villages were invaded, and by the 1980s their narrow winding streets were painted with double yellow lines to forbid parking.

Meanwhile, the larger Victorian resorts have had to follow fashion as far as they can. A problem for them was always that they were

BELOW: *Waiting at Paddington for the train to Devon in 1922 when the south-west was still exclusive. Railway companies found it hard to meet the demand for travel to the seaside, especially on Bank Holidays.*

RIGHT: *The beach has always induced a kind of silliness which is part of the liberating effect of a seaside holiday.*

overwhelmed for a few weeks in the year, then empty out of season. The habit of retiring to the sea has brought a more steady prosperity to some resorts, but the pattern of a migrant labour force continues. A good deal of the holiday atmosphere has gone, as the seaside has become a popular place for conferences. The saddest loss since the fortunes of the old resorts have waned is the Regency and Victorian architecture. Sea air is not only bracing, it is corrosive as is the desire to remain in fashion.

This makes the wonderfully rich photographic record of the resorts that much more valuable and evocative. It goes back far enough to capture the bathing machines on the beach, the seafronts before the promenades were built and the hotels stretched out from what had been villages, or little towns, all jostling for that magical position – a sea view. In the railway age the resorts were boom towns, at one period growing faster than any other of the rapidly expanding Victorian cities.

For those who today are forced to endure the congestion and tedium of the airport on their way to a fortnight's frying in the sun, the following account of the first Bank Holiday in 1871, from *The News of the World*, might be some consolation:

'From 8 a.m. the cry at every railway station was 'Still they come!' and the supply of passengers very far exceeds the supply of accommodation. At Fenchurch Street Station there was a crowd of hundreds struggling for tickets to Margate and Southend ... Margate Jetty was simply blocked so far as to be impassable, whilst thousands of excursionists who came down by rail wandered along the cliffs. ... The people arrived at Cannon Street and Charing Cross for Ramsgate at 8 a.m. and it was 10 o'clock before the surprised but very active officials at the South Eastern could accommodate all their passengers ... It was simply impossible to get to the seaside.'

BELOW: *Seaside fun at Clacton in the 1920s.*

THE JOURNEY

Until the 1960s, a trip to the seaside began for most people at a railway station. By the 1930s, the exodus to the coast in the peak summer months and on Bank Holidays was such that it was considered a serious problem by the railway companies. Holiday travel by train had increased three times between the 1920s and the 1930s. There were efforts to persuade employers to stagger the holiday season, and to encourage people to go to the less popular resorts. Before the system collapsed under the weight of shrimp nets and buckets and spades, the war intervened, and though railway travel to the sea revived in the late 1940s and 1950s more and more people were going by car, and introducing the new problem – the Bank Holiday traffic jam.

RIGHT: *A genteel gathering of holidaymakers waiting expectantly at Paddington in 1924 for the Cornish Riviera Express.*

BELOW: *Weighing the children at Waterloo station on the Londoner's great day out to the south coast on August Bank holiday in 1913.*

LEFT: *A party of serious, well-to-do holidaymakers at Paddington station in 1910. It was only the relatively well off who could afford a week or two at the seaside in this period; and they escaped, if they could, to the relative peace of West Country resorts.*

ABOVE: *Another classic Edwardian station scene at Paddington in 1910.*

The Company Outing

Even in the 1930s, a day trip to the seaside was the most a great many working people could expect. Railway companies had early on recognized the value of the excursion train with cheap fares. In 1841 Thomas Cook founded the now famous travel agents, with an excursion train for temperance supporters from Leicester to Loughborough. It was the equivalent of the airlines' charter flights. As these photographs suggest, however, most trippers did *not* go to the coast to sing hymns and abstain from liquor.

RIGHT: *The annual trip to Margate in 1935 for employees of Carreras, the cigarette company.*

TOP: *More girls from Carreras' 'Black Cat Club' (Black Cat was a brand of cigarette).*

BOTTOM: *Employees from Woolwich Arsenal Co-operative on their way to Margate in 1931.*

LEFT: *An exceptionally cheerful family party setting off from Paddington in 1923 – this stage of the annual holiday was usually beset with anxiety.*

ABOVE: *High jinks down at Canvey Island on the Thames estuary as a carload of swells head for the beach in 1923.*

BOARD AND LODGING

The burgeoning seaside resorts of the Victorian period were built fast, but never fast enough to keep up with demand. At places like Blackpool people slept four or five to a bed. Few could afford the luxury of the big hotels which spread along the seafront. Throughout the history of the seaside, complaints have been made about bad accommodation and dreadful food. The seaside landlady became a figure of modern folk myth. It was because the South African showman Billy Butlin was so appalled by his treatment in a British seaside resort that he set up his first holiday camps, where at least there was something to do in bad weather and a permanent place to stay.

METROPOLE AND GRAND HOTE

RIGHT: *The height of luxury – the Metropole and Grand Hotel, Brighton*

RIGHTON.

A popular solution to the problem of where to stay on the coast was the caravan.

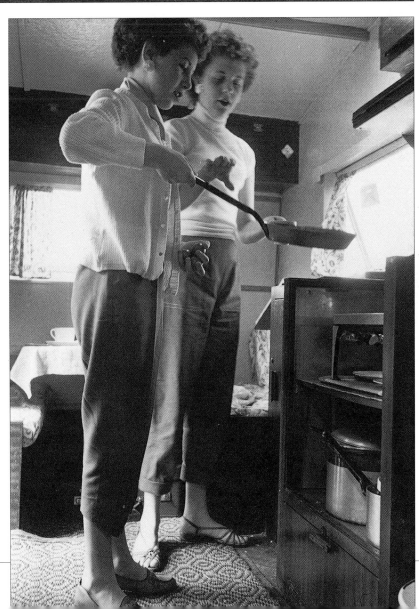

TOP LEFT: *An early example, equipped with 'fishing rod' radio aerial, at Leigh-on-Sea in Essex in 1926 – a favourite area for East Londoners.*

BOTTOM LEFT: *A more up-to-date version from the 1950s, its lady occupants proudly – if somewhat precariously – posed alongside.*

ABOVE: *One would have thought the trees would have provided enough shade for these 1930s picnickers – but protocol had to be observed and the parasol set up.*

RIGHT: *A caravan fry-up during Blackpool's Wakes Week, the annual summer holiday for mill town workers.*

RIGHT: *There were two hundred holiday camps in Britain just before the Second World War. One of the newest was the neon-lit Prestatyn 'chalet village' opened by Thomas Cook in 1939. This form of mass luxury was much frowned upon by the serious rock-pool brigades of Cornwall, but in the years just after the war holiday camps were relatively up-market.*

ABOVE: *A 'holiday uncle' directs holidaymakers arriving at Prestatyn in 1947 when, for a brief period, middle-class people still infused with the social solidarity of wartime were happy to go to holiday camps.*

ABOVE: *A cheerful 'Hi-dee-hi' in 1955 from the most celebrated of holiday-camp characters, Butlin's 'red coats'. These fun police are on duty at Skegness in Lincolnshire where Billy Butlin built his first camp in 1936.*

HOMELANDS
OFFER

SPACIOUS LOUNGES
TENNIS · BILLIARDS
& DANCE ROOMS.
AIR RAID SHELTER
LIFT · NIGHT PORTER

Excellent Cuisine

REASONABLE TERMS

ABOVE: *The war did not do away with seaside holidays altogether. Here the Brighton hoteliers and landladies prepare for visitors in November 1941.*

LEFT: *The search for seaside 'digs'. Many families slept in one room, buying their own food which the landlady cooked and served.*

LEFT: *That archetypal figure, the seaside landlady – Mrs Chegwidden of Newquay, in 1952.*

BELOW: *Another Newquay landlady serves a guest-house family in 1952, a time when rising prices – and changing tastes – were making life harder for these stalwarts of the seaside holiday.*

TAKING THE PLUNGE

Fewer and fewer people these days are prepared to brave the cold waters of the North Sea, the Channel or the Atlantic once they have enjoyed the tepid Mediterranean. Fewer still would be prepared to start the day drinking a couple of pints of sea water as the health enthusiast did in the eighteenth century. But splashing around on the edge of an outgoing or incoming tide has always been considered fun.

As with so much which becomes regarded as pleasurable, the sea was first recommended by doctors as a cure for almost anything. The most celebrated work was *A Dissertation concerning the Use of Sea-Water in Diseases of the Glands*, published in the 1750s by Dr Richard Russell. It was in the last years of the Victorian period that swimming became really popular, often in sea-water public pools built on the coast. From this the modern, functional costume evolved. The logical conclusion is to bathe naked as did the eighteenth-century pioneers. Brighton has revived a nudist beach where, in the early nineteenth century, guidebooks warned the unwary vistor they might see heathen swimmers plunging stark naked into the sea.

RIGHT: *Bathing belles at Bexhill-on-Sea in the 1920s. The idea of 'getting a tan' was just becoming fashionable with the upper crust in this period.*

LEFT: *A formidable beach party from around 1880, none of whom looks likely to strip off and tear into the sea with abandon.*

ABOVE: *A classic picture by Paul Martin of day trippers testing the water on August Bank Holiday in 1892. Paddling was a popular alternative to bathing for those who could not afford bathing machines or costumes.*

RIGHT: *This is the kind of scene that enraged Victorian moralists. The seaside air has induced these ladies to show more than was regarded as decent. But this was 1902 and not quite as shocking as it once was.*

FAR RIGHT: *Fashions were changing just before the outbreak of the Great War. This holidaymaker at Gorleston in July 1914 has a changing tent rather than a bathing machine, and a functional, almost modern-looking costume.*

BELOW: *Scarborough, former spa and one of the longest established seaside resorts, in the summer of 1913. This was where the first bathing machines were used in the eighteenth century. The resort has attracted quite a mix of social classes from the north of England.*

BELOW: *Amateur and professional fishermen have always mingled at the seaside. Behind the anglers casting from the front at Scarborough in 1913 is a fishing boat.*

TOP RIGHT: *An old sea dog spins a yarn to a ready audience of trippers on the seafont in 1910.*

BOTTOM RIGHT: *A brisk trade at the bait shop on Brighton Pier in 1950.*

Shrimping

For the upper crust interested in nature and biology, seaside crustacea were an endless source of fascination: collecting specimens was both enjoyable and educational. Rock-pooling and shrimping remain one of the great pleasures of the coast in those places where the marine life has survived the poisons of anti-fouling paint on boats.

RIGHT: *A classic shrimping pose struck by fashionable bathers around 1910.*

BELOW: Punch *magazine satirized the stooped figures of shrimpers and shell collectors as a strange form of sea creature. These 1913 shrimpers are hunched on Scarborough beach.*

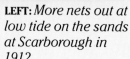

LEFT: *More nets out at low tide on the sands at Scarborough in 1912.*

ABOVE: *Naturally, a great many fishing villages were transformed into seaside resorts in the nineteenth century. These fishermen are from Leigh-on-Sea on the Thames estuary which still has a small fleet today.*

TOP: *A cockle lady of Stiffkey (pronounced Stewkey) in Norfolk, a parish which became notorious in the inter-war years for its licentious vicar.*

ABOVE: *A fine view of Whitby around the turn of the century. This was once a great whaling station and a shipbuilding town in the days of sail when it made many of the colliers which carried coals to London. The town resisted the tide of tourism longer than some but bowed in the end to the railway and the tripper.*

LEFT: *Bathers at Southsea at the turn of the century. The bathing machine, in which those taking the plunge changed into their costumes and were wheeled out into the sea, would soon be no more.*

RIGHT: *Little Johnnie at Lulworth in August 1910. Many families have treasured holiday snapshots like this one.*

BELOW: *A fine panorama of the beach at Skegness in Edwardian times. The most striking feature is the density of the crowds and the amount of clothing they are wearing. A sun tan was not then a sign of health or distinction.*

Lulworth Aug 1910

Johnnie

BELOW: *A trio from Plymouth Ladies Swimming Club in 1924.*

ABOVE: *A heatwave at Broadstairs in the twenties entices a jolly party into the sea. Having your photograph taken was all part of the fun.*

ABOVE: *No bathing machines for this quartet emerging in liberated twenties costumes from their first dip of the holiday. Broadstairs in 1928.*

Yachting

Yachting was always a very exclusive way of
enjoying the seaside. At all periods, some
people have sailed for pleasure, but yachting
as it is known today dates from around the
early nineteenth century. The word 'yacht'
comes from the Dutch, *jaght*, meaning a cargo
or war ship converted to a pleasure boat. The
early yachting clubs would race and practise
manouevres – there was a touch of naval
training about it. These people take the sea
seriously and yachting has not been invaded
by what is regarded as the vulgarity of the
seaside resort.

BELOW: *A splendidly
turned-out crew at
Cowes Regatta in the
1930s.*

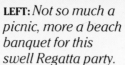

LEFT: *Not so much a
picnic, more a beach
banquet for this
swell Regatta party.*

ABOVE: *The arrival of the Royal Yacht for Cowes Regatta on the Isle of Wight in 1921. The Royal Yacht Squadron was formed in 1804 to practice manouevres – it was the year before Trafalgar. In 1815, the Royal Yacht Club was formed; it began to meet at Cowes in the 1820s. Under royal patronage the now internationally famous Cowes Regatta began to emerge in the 1830s.*

LEFT: *A boat trip is part of the fun of the seaside. You wouldn't think so to look at this Victorian family.*

BELOW: *Fishermen offer trips in their boats at turn-of-the-century Skegness.*

BOTTOM: *Things look much jollier in this fine view of pleasure boats in Bridlington harbour.*

The changing face of the British seaside in the inter-war years.

ABOVE: *A glamorous line-up of the winning team of the Ladies' Spade Race at Shanklin on the Isle of Wight in 1932.*

TOP LEFT: *There is hardly room to move on the beach at Southend-on-Sea in August 1935.*

BOTTOM LEFT: *One of the last of the old bathing-machine attendants on Brighton beach.*

RIGHT: *An ice-cream seller in waders serves two girls in revealing swimwear at Brighton in August 1939.*

By the 1950s, skimpy swimwear and the bikini – named, bizarrely, after the islands where the Americans tested the atomic bomb – had arrived. As with all fashions, these suited some women better than others.

RIGHT: *Sitting it out at Margate in 1951.*

BELOW: *Breasting the waves with confidence at Eastbourne, also in 1951.*

OPPOSITE TOP: *A quick paddle, fully clothed, was still preferred by some people at Blackpool in 1956.*

OPPOSITE BOTTOM: *Children performing the familiar conjuring trick of changing under a towel during a summer of dreadful weather at Bournemouth in1954.*

THE BEACH

It is remarkable how attractive people find a sandy beach, even when they are fully clothed, for it is liable to produce a gritty discomfort. However, the appeal of the beach has endured and sand has proved to be a very versatile material, and the great open space when the tide is out an irresistible natural stage set for many kinds of entertainment. This perhaps has something to do with the fact that mass tourism arose in the latter part of the nineteenth century, when about 80 per cent of British people lived in cramped and dirty towns. In the end, of course, the popularity of the beach defeated its great appeal, for at peak times it became as cramped and dirty as the towns people had escaped from. But the seaside retained at least the bracing air and that special determination to find enjoyment somehow.

RIGHT: *The sea has disappeared from view at low tide on Blackpool beach at the turn of the century, leaving a vast expanse of sand which is being sculpted into a great variety of hills and castles.*

LEFT: *A wonderful image of the seaside in the era before sunbathing became fashionable. This is Southsea in the 1890s, with what looks like a school outing in the foreground.*

BELOW: *Aimless strolling is one of the favourite pastimes on the beach. These young holidaymakers are among the crowds on Whitby beach in 1913.*

RIGHT: *A cavalry charge of kilted soldiers at Brighton. The donkey ride, a favourite with children, also allowed adults in a boisterous mood to make an ass of themselves.*

BELOW: *A fine portrait of a posse of youngsters at Ramsgate in 1905, by the renowned photographer, Paul Martin.*

BELOW: *Slow business for the donkey man at Scarborough during the Second World War.*

Entertainers have always followed the crowds, and the tradition that included music hall and film stars appearing at the seaside has continued into the age of television. In seaside rep. you can *see the stars* for real.

TOP RIGHT: *On a duller Southsea day in the same period, musicians try to draw a crowd.*

LEFT: *In the past, there were many entertainments on the beach: Punch and Judy shows, clowns, comedians, and small bands. At Southsea in the 1890s (where someone has put up an umbrella against the bright sun), two entertainers appear to be blacked up like the ever popular 'nigger minstrels'.*

BOTTOM RIGHT: *These clowns or pierrots are performing on a portable stage at Scarborough in 1907.*

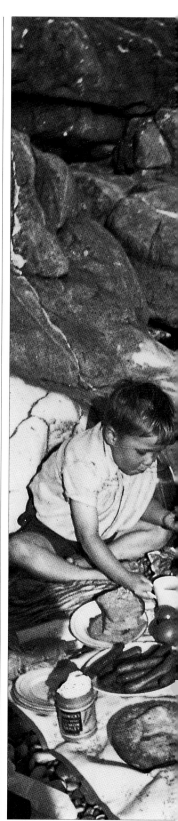

*Another timeless pleasure of the seaside –
eating* al fresco.

ABOVE: *Tucking in on the sand at Great
Yarmouth in 1913.*

RIGHT: *A feast in the shingle somewhere on the
Welsh coast in the post-war years.*

BELOW: *A smart-looking hamper lunch served
on the cliffs of Llandudno in North Wales in
1935.*

Some stalwart and determined children braving the stiff breezes of the English coast in a pursuit of pleasure that seems timeless.

ABOVE: *Leaning into the breeze on the sands of Bamburgh on the north-east coast around 1910.*

LEFT: *Holding onto one's hat at Southsea in the 1890s.*

RIGHT: *A brave smile from the girl without the headscarf in her sandboat at Newquay in Cornwall, probably in the 1940s.*

LEFT: *Felixstowe in 1928, and the first unsociable signs of personal portable sound systems have arrived with the wind-up gramophone. In time, this would evolve into the blaring transistor radio.*

RIGHT: *It was in the twenties that beachwear fashion favoured the figure that needed no flattery and the flapper could parade like a mannequin on the strand. These two posers were snapped at Margate.*

LEFT: *Lowestoft, 1926. Smoking in public, another new fashion for ladies, gives these two bathers a very modern look.*

ABOVE: *Yet more activity on the ever versatile beach: a family cricket match on the sands of Embleton Bay on the north-east coast in the summer of 1913.*

BELOW: *Perhaps the management is at the other end of this rope robustly held by ladies on a factory outing to Hastings in 1925.*

LEFT: *This looks as if it might be a classic seaside summer scene: it is, in fact, February 1925 at Brighton. Enthusiasts from the local swimming club take advantage of a spell of mild weather.*

BELOW: *What happened next we do not know, but the feet of the naval rating and his companion look perilously close to the rope. Jersey in 1935.*

RIGHT: *The ultimate in mixed bathing – a piggyback down to the sea, with ladies in the saddle. Note the line of bathing tents in the background. Shanklin on the Isle of Wight, 1928.*

RIGHT: *Where the only beach was a rocky cove, as here on the coast of Cornwall at Trebarwith, the fun fairs and day trippers were kept away and sensitive souls could soak up the scenery – until the ubiquitous motor car arrived.*

LEFT: *Last of the halcyon days for the secluded village of St Ives in Cornwall, famous for its colony of seaside artists. Another view of the harbour at low tide goes on to canvas in 1948.*

BELOW: *The idyllic clustered village of Looe in Cornwall.*

Wartime Beaches

During the Second World War, the seaside was transformed. Beaches on the south and east coasts were heavily fortified against invasion, while the less vulnerable resorts such as Blackpool were turned into military camps. Southend Pier became a naval base, and many other resorts took into their empty accommodation civil servants from the cities. Many evacuated children went to the coast too, some for the first time in their lives.

LEFT: *August 1939 on Brighton beach, with the rumble of war in Europe getting louder. But even then nobody knew what was in store, and that soon this would be the front line.*

ABOVE: *Even in wartime, there was some fun on the beach. In 1943 these Land Girls hitch-hiked to an unidentified coastal location to spend Easter by the sea.*

LEFT: *The classic British holiday by the sea – Bournemouth in 1954, just before people started to escape to the warmth of the Mediterranean. What is striking is the determination to stay on the beach whatever the weather.*

BELOW: *Nothing is so poignant as the seaside out of season: a nicely posed deckchair against a backdrop of shuttered beach bars and ice-cream stands at Portsmouth.*

RIGHT: *This shot of a bathing attendant at Worthing in 1935 takes some explaining. Has he caught the child trying to steal a deckchair? Or is he about to teach her to swim?*

ABOVE: *Temperance trips to the seaside were common in the Victorian period – Thomas Cook began his travel agent's business by organizing an excursion for his own group. A preacher on the beach was more rare, and by the middle of this century probably an endangered species. This open-air service was at Weston-super-mare in 1949.*

RIGHT: *Torquay, which unwisely claimed the title of the 'British Riviera' in the 1950s.*

Maybe, after all, the essence of the seaside and the beach has not changed all that much since the last century.

ABOVE: *This breezy party were having fun at Canvey Island in 1923*

LEFT: *This remarkable photograph was taken at Yarmouth in the 1890s.*

ON THE PROM

The rising tide of seaside holidaymakers from the early nineteenth century onwards swamped the existing coastal towns and very soon they had to build new sea walls and defences. On top of these, visitors would promenade, and what was created out of necessity became a planned feature of the popular resorts in later years. The other term for 'The Prom' – the Esplanade – comes from French *esplaner*, to level out, which is what the developers did to the coastline.

Piers began as landing stages for boats which would otherwise not be able to operate at low tide or where there was no good harbour. One or two resorts had piers as early as 1800, but the peak period for building them was in the late nineteenth century, by which time they had become an extension of the prom and a great attraction in their own right, carrying above the sea fun-palaces and dance halls. It became customary to charge landbound tourists to go onto piers which became big money-spinners for the resorts. But piers were always expensive to build and maintain, and many on the south and east coasts were badly damaged in the last war. Where they survive they still give that pleasant feeling of going to sea while remaining on dry land.

RIGHT: *A wonderful view of Scarborough's sweeping Esplanade around 1911, with holidaymakers promenading.*

THE PIER, SOUTHEND-ON-SEA.

2003.

LEFT: *The pier to end all piers at Southend-on-Sea, a landmark for which the pleasure steamers from London would race to arrive first and take on passengers for the return trip. Southend's first wooden pier of the 1830s was replaced by the existing one in the 1890s.*

BELOW: *This splendid photograph of Southsea in the 1890s by F. J. Mortimer provides a nice illustration of the original function of the pier – to provide a landing place for steamers.*

DAILY TELEGRAPH
LARGEST CIRCULATION IN THE WORLD

LANDPORT DRAPERY BAZAAR
DRESSES MILLINERY AND MANTLES

ABOVE: *Across the prom and into the sea. Two very modern bathing belles at Porthcawl, the Welsh resort, in 1939. Beachwear has always looked out of place on the Esplanade.*

RIGHT: *A proper promenade at Blackpool in 1955 during Wakes Week, the annual holiday for Lancashire mill workers.*

Once the piers and promenades were built, the entertainment industry was able to shift lock, stock and barrel to the seaside resorts during the summer season.

The outdoors often had to be taken indoors, for rain was not unknown during the seaside holiday. A light and airy haven, perhaps with a view of the tempest raging outside, was an essential feature of the resort from early on.

ABOVE: *A tea dance at Blackpool.*

RIGHT: *Live music on Brighton Pier in 1950.*

RIGHT: *The gentleman in the tea-rooms at Westcliff-on-Sea around 1910 looks as if he might imagine himself aboard ship.*

BELOW: *The floral hall on the Parade at Bridlington in 1919.*

Carnivals

Once the promenades were built, they became
a stage on which resorts could attract the
crowds with a variety of events. Between the
wars, the most popular seaside towns spent
millions on their seafronts: Blackpool invested
one and a half million pounds. Many resorts
held carnivals of one kind or another, electing
their Queens who would be paraded through
the town and along the promenade in the peak
of the season. Resorts, in many ways, become
just like other towns with a life derived more
from the culture of industrial regions inland
than from the seafaring traditions of their
origins.

LEFT: *A more modest affair than Blackpool's, Gravesend Carnival nevertheless had its Queen. She is about to start a race of delivery men.*

BOTTOM LEFT: *Another view of the 1930 Blackpool carnival.*

BELOW: *Elected Britain's Cotton Queen from eighteen contending Lancashire Cotton Queens, Miss F. Locke leads the carnival procession along Blackpool's promenade in 1930.*

ABOVE: *The Great Wheel and Winter Gardens at Blackpool – famous features of the development of the resort between the wars.*

BELOW: *Brighton Pier in 1950. The lady trying her luck at darts is a soprano, Josette Adrienne, who was appearing at Brighton's Grand Theatre. She looks in fine voice here.*

ABOVE: *The posed line-up of ladies on the pier have lost interest in the sea view: the one on the left has paid one old penny to watch 'Her Hubby Sweetie'.*

LEFT: *Brighton's Palace Pier in August 1946, restored to its peacetime popularity.*

BELOW: *Eastbourne's pier, like many others on the south coast, was partially demolished during the war as an anti-invasion measure. Here, in the wet March of 1947, the machines are being restored for the new season.*

ABOVE: *Not a greasy pole contest but an enterprising exercise in floral civic pride at Folkstone in 1936. The seafront flower bed is tended by two gardeners who have improvised a scaffold to reach the central blooms without damaging their lovingly tended creation.*

LEFT: *A health check – part of the seaside tradition – on Blackpool's promenade in 1955.*

LEFT: *The horse-drawn tram, a mainstay of cheap public transport in New York and London at the end of the nineteenth century, still has a function at Douglas on the Isle of Man. Holidaymakers are being hauled along the seafront in 1937.*

BELOW: *The bandstand on Eastbourne seafront in 1950, during the last great boom period for British holiday resorts.*

BELOW: *Tea, that other great British institution, was never far away on a traditional seaside holiday.*

RIGHT: *Cockles, mussels, winkles ... Shellfish stalls like this are rare now, in the age of the ubiquitous hamburger bar.*

BELOW: *It used to be called Hokey Pokey. Ice cream and the sea go together. Brighton Pier in the 1950s.*

ABOVE: *Homeward bound – asleep with bucket and spade.*